Letters, To The Men I Have Loved

Mirtha Michelle Castro Mármol

Outskirts Press, Inc.
Denver, Colorado

For Anthony Jules &
Angel de Jesus Mármol

CONTENTS

PREFACE

I don't want to encourage your tears.
I simply want to help you feel.
To make you feel alive,
in a world in which the days have become routine,
and your best kisses replay in your memory,
like faded dreams.

When thinking of a title for this book I originally contemplated in titling it *"Becoming a Woman"*. It is my belief that a woman is not only birthed, a woman is made. A girl becomes a woman through experiences. A journey that will release tears, develop patience, maturity, independence and most importantly a strong sense of self. I know there are many more stories I have yet to live but until now this book is a part of my story. I decided on the title when I was writing a chapter and I felt I was writing an ex-lover a letter. Writing to him things I never expressed in person, but had to write in order to release him from my soul. When you develop a strong bond with someone your souls kiss in the spiritual realm. When it's time to move forward, that *"kiss"* or what many want to call *"connection"* must be broken. It doesn't occur from one day to another. It takes healing like anything once it breaks.

I also realized that writing was my release mechanism since my first disillusionment as a little girl. I wrote to release the emotions I bottled up as result of the strength my mother instilled in me. To release pain and to express my joy, I wrote. Sometimes I wrote in journals and in little napkins at restaurants. I even wrote on the palm of my hand. Every word in this book I birthed in solitude or in pain. Sometimes it was under the influence of wine or under the influence of hate, and sometimes under harsh sobriety. We all prefer to talk about love. In my opinion hate is just as powerful and influential in the human life. No one wants to admit they hate because since children we are taught that hate is ugly and love is beautiful. But to recognize love sometimes one must at some point experience how horrible hate feels. The same goes with happiness, gratitude, strength, and pain. All these emotions rule the roller coaster we call life and we should not be afraid to feel each and every one of them. To feel was the biggest gift our creator gave us and our entire human journey will depend on emotions.

I personally don't have the authority to tell anyone how to live his or her life. I can't tell you how to love or be loved. How to respect yourself or how to be respected. I can't tell you how to talk, how to walk, or how to eat, but I can tell you I myself have made many mistakes. Some things I'm ashamed to admit. If it weren't for those mistakes I wouldn't have seen the beauty within me. I wouldn't have awoken the goddess that lives in me. You see, goddesses although immortal were all flawed. They were all a bit extreme at their calling, and they were all betrayed and hurt at some point. Some were even considered devious, but what made them unique was their strength. They did not give up. Their circumstances did not deter them from their purpose or bestowing their gifts to humans. Whether it was the gift of Love, Art, Wisdom, Family, Intelligence, Beauty or War. They gave gifts to whomever they encountered. I pray that my mistakes, my loves and my pains be turned into gifts. I pray those gifts serve as motivation that there is strength in each of us, no matter how big the ordeal has been. I pray my gifts live as myths in words with whomever I encounter, and for my words to live beyond the chambers of mortality in each of your hearts. I present you *"Letters, To The Men I Have Loved"* because regardless of how distant these men and I might have become and how many years have passed by, I lived their laughs, their passions, their failures, and their successes. This book of letters and poetry are the feelings they evoked in me.

Genuinely,
Mirtha Michelle Castro Mármol

When I see you,
I can't help
But be reminded
Of all the mountains
We didn't move,
Of all the things I didn't do.
The odds are against us,
There is nothing left,
But my desire,
To immortalize you in words.

LETTER I

If I can't have you near me,
I will write you in my nights.
I will paint with words a vivid picture,
Of how it feels to have you
by my side.

Lust

If only I could have filmed our last night, and rewatch the lust we experienced. If only I could transfer the mental photograph I currently have of your eyes staring into mine into a physical one. If only I can scream to the world the sensation I felt when you rapidly pulled me close to you and kissed me for me not to leave your side. If only you could understand how I did not want to leave and secretly hoped for you to do exactly what you did. You pushed on me against the wall as you dug your fingers in my hair, like only you know how to do. Kissed me so passionately that there was no choice but to proceed. Proceed to what we have done so well, since the first time destiny brought us together. There was no time to walk to neither a bed nor a couch. It had to happen in that exact furious moment. A moment in which we both deep inside knew would be our last time, because what we were doing was absolutely wrong. Wrong in everyone's eyes but no one was watching. Only your cold wood floor witnessed our heat. In that moment my only desire was to kiss every part of you, even your shadow–*and I did*. I kissed you as a woman who has nothing to lose. A woman who for years loved you, sometimes openly and sometimes in silence.

I kissed you exactly how I wanted you to remember me. Remember me for the passion we lived. Remember me for our heat. The heat that we have tried to hide every time we happen to cross paths, but remains obvious underneath it all.

If there is such thing as a sexual soulmate, I must admit you were my first. On numerous occasions I dwelled on this idea. Especially after knowing you for so many years. It is said that when soulmates meet there is an unspoken understanding of one another, and when they lay with each other there is no greater joy than that. Something special occurred when our bodies came together. A certain alchemy that confirmed we knew each other in a previous time, and that Alchemy made lovemaking with you easy. I still remember our first time as it was yesterday. I actually still remember the sensation of when your lips first touched mine. It was an unfamiliar ecstasy, and my first brush with that kind of chemistry. There was never an awkward moment that sometimes new lovers experience. No asking what I liked or what you liked because we knew. Something about the way we moved together. I could never resist you. One look from you and every other man I met became history.

I always blamed timing on our love story never reaching its full potential. I wasn't ready when you were ready, and you didn't trust me when I was ready. I never opened myself completely to you. I genuinely didn't know how to, partly because of fear. I was young and although I didn't fear falling in love, I feared losing myself to love. So we lived a reckless love story filled with games, jealousy and sometimes spite. So many times I screamed at you and you screamed at me, only to end up between sheets like two pride-less animals. It was a kind of lust that is difficult to describe, and I cannot understand why time hasn't dimmed it. You brought out a certain sexuality in me, which at times felt sinful. Sex with you became addicting. I craved your sex and I dreamt of our chemistry. *I wonder if that type of passion could survive monogamy. I wonder had we formed a family, whether that passion would have survived?*

Our lives became a game of being consumed by that passion, then most of the time keeping it dormant in our bodies until it exploded the moment when we found each other alone. One evening we both fell into the trap again. We chased each other like cat and mouse until we ended up in a house far away somewhere making out like teenagers in a desolate kitchen. You took me on the granite counter. Your sex entered me. It had been years and nothing had changed. You missed me. Your mouth said it but your sex also proved it. You needed me in your life as I needed you in mine. Even if it was from far away, we still needed each other. I needed to know you were fine, and you needed to know I was content, even if it was with another man. As your sex thrust inside of me I forgot about how different our lives were. In that moment there was only you, and my desire to feel one more time how it felt to be in your arms again. *Because the reality is I never, for one moment, ever stopped loving you.*

After we did the inevitable there you sat on the kitchen counter staring at me with those eyes that I had loved so much. A mellow brown and certain vulnerability resides in them. Eyes in which melt my heart, because I seemed to always see the good in you. In that moment your mouth bespoke the words your eyes always said. You said I was the woman you had the most passion for and that would never change. My desire was to kiss you all over again, and to commit the most beautiful and meaningful sin with you again. How should making love to your soulmate ever be considered a sin?

Outside of the lust, in my heart I truly loved you. I will always love you. A love in which I know is real because I never stopped wanting the best for you, even when I felt you hated me. You expressed to feel a certain "*love-hate*" for me at some point. My only conclusion for that was that you indeed loved me, but you hated me because you couldn't trust me. I lost your trust in a way only you and I know, but you must understand that only occurred as a result of what you had done first. When a man feels betrayed it's the end of all things. Without asking themselves what did they themselves do for it to get to that point? Years after you opened up to me and confessed you still loved me, and it took you some time but you eventually understood we *BOTH* made mistakes. My heart sunk a little. It sunk because some realizations occur too late, and ultimately only the lovers suffers.

I Miss My Lover

Could it be that our souls
At some point became entwined,
And it was inconceivable
That we would
Ever part?
Could it be that I played with fire?
And these burns,
Were the price I had to pay?
Scabs of spite I could have avoided,
If only I would have stayed away.
But how could I have avoided
The touch that only you possess?
Chemistry so strong,
That only storybooks can illustrate.
I desire your kisses,
Like a drought needs the rain.
I close my eyes to relive our last embrace,
And cannot help,
But wonder who you will love next.

My Secret

I always spoke of our future ending,
In truth,
I never believed in a possible end.
Apparently my words have power,
And like Midas' wish of the gold touch,
My words became reality.
It's over and done,
That's what the song says,
It's over and done,
That's what your heart says,
But mine-
My heart can't take it.
My imagination runs wild,
At the thought that tonight,
You will be another's.
My fear grows at the thought,
That you will possibly love her,
Like my kisses before,
You will hold her.
And our story will be left
To perish in the darkness,
Shut In secrecy,
Because till this day,
We still deny each other.

You and I

In the night while they sleep,
When the birds don't shriek,
You and I become one.

One look I cannot resist,
A single touch I do desire.
I crave the fruit of your tree.
Never did sin taste this sweet.

My sweet,
Why should I be called a thief?
When a man like you,
Is free as a summer wind.

A friend or foe,
What has she become?
Consider I their single careless night,
Or her many pluckings,
Should I revise?

Saint she is not,
Neither us in disguise,
But in the night,
Closer to God we are.
Side by side,
Secret Lovers,
That's you and I.

But, We Danced

We danced many moons ago.
Not a Waltz, Not a Tango,
But we danced.
Your fingertips coyly engaged with mine.
A soulful recognition occurred,
Between our eyes,
Both hearts.
Beating, as you and I danced.
Not a Waltz, Not a Tango,
But we danced.

I Haven't Learned

I have learned about philosophy,
And about meditating alone
Under a cloudless sky.
I have learned about metals and stones,
And what makes them shine.
I have learned about the intricacies
Of tasting and decanting wine.
I have learned about mythological figures,
And how they fought with pride.
I have learned about the eagle,
And how it soars alone so high.
I have learned about energy,
And how it can't be destroyed,
But can change form over time.
I have learned about wisdom,
From Solomon's Proverbs,
And about soft brush strokes
From impressionist paintings.
I have learned plenty
About worldly pleasures,
And diving alone into dark oceans,
But I still haven't learned
How to act when I see you.
How to stop the adrenaline rush
I feel–*when I breathe you.*
How to calm my heart,
When I hear you,
And how to bury my frustration,
Of the impossibility of once again–*being with you.*

LETTER II

When I think about love
my thoughts begin
and end with you.

Love

Every ounce of joy I felt had been robbed from me was returned to my life the moment I first held you in my arms. Your perfect little fingers, and perfect toes, and chubby little thighs were a piece of heaven in the disaster that was my life then. I was so young and confused, and all I did was dream and pray for a life I felt I was destined to live in Los Angeles. I partied my nights away in the decadence of South Beach. I drank champagne as if it was water, and always left room for the vodka. When you were born it's as if life made a little more sense. As if I understood why I still lived in Miami. For you were the reason I had to be there. Your mom wasn't necessarily ready to have you, and as her sister I felt I had to step up and be there for her. As young girls we played house and we talked about getting married and having a family with the perfect house, and the perfect husband. Unfortunately, life wasn't as perfect for her. Within her mistakes as a young woman–*she was brave.* When certain people suggested for her to terminate the pregnancy, she unselfishly became reluctant to that idea. Both your parents decided to keep you. Daddy didn't talk to her for months after he found out she was pregnant. I know he was hurting. It wasn't very acceptable in our family to have a child out of wedlock, but then one day he came around and felt her belly and you kicked. He felt the fire in you he said, and that day he nicknamed you "Pyro", meaning fire in Greek. That's exactly what you are for us. You are the fire that lit our family. You are the light that brightens our lives.

I became like your second mommy. She would go to work, and even with my hangovers I took care of you. I fed you and changed your diapers. I told you stories and put you to sleep. And in that process a zealousness built inside of me for you. I needed to protect you. I needed to accomplish my dreams so I could give you the things your mother sometimes lacked. Although blood is strong hearts aren't stolen, hearts are given, and I gave you my heart. It was a higher level of love. One that was unknown to me until you were born. The type of love God has for his children, an unconditional type of love.

Eventually, I packed my bags and moved out West. You were a year old, and already learning how to walk. I was excited for my new life, but the one thing that kept me down was the idea I was going to miss out on so many moments of your life. It didn't matter I often visited Miami, I was still missing those little moments that would never be the same through Skype. I'll never forgive myself for that. Maybe that's why I try to stay so present in your life. It was so exciting when you were speaking fluently and you could express to me the happenings of your day. Now you amaze me even more. Your vocabulary is impressive for your young age. Your intelligence and comprehension is one to boast on. To the point you deserve gold, because you are gold.

It is my hope that when you look at yourself in the mirror you won't see what people say you are. Yes, you are Latino. Yes, you have milk colored skin, and the most beautiful full lips. It is my hope you can always see beyond your big brown eyes, and beyond the resemblance of your mother and father combined. I need you to see beyond and always see yourself as *GOLD*. Never be constrained by your environment or what anyone sees or not sees in you, because all that should matter is that you see *GOLD*. For you are and will be a winner in everything you do. Remember there are no losses, because if God did not grant you a desire it is simply because it was not written. Never doubt in yourself, as you should never doubt in your destiny.

Any accomplishments in my life were never greater than when you accomplished something. Every time you won a baseball game, voted MVP, won a Karate championship, your amazing school grades, your high reading scores. Those are always my proudest moments. You are gifted, you are a child of the sun, my perfect child, my inspiration derives from you. I am proud and blessed to be your aunt. You forever own my smile, and will always have my utmost unconditional love.

Before You

Before you everything was tainted,
in the most average colors.
My palette lacked
All those infusions
Your mere presence offers.
Like a child,
I can paint all the hues of your pupils,
When the light strikes.
And nothing compares to the smile that you bring me,
The moment I catch a glimpse
Of your large expressive eyes.

LETTER III

If my words fail,
let my eyes and my heart
be my language.

Wisdom

There is not a day I do not think of you. I miss your soft hands and the way you would move them as you spoke., as if they were whimsically floating in air. I loved combing your white perfect hair. I miss the depth of your large blue eyes. I miss you on your rocking chair and all the stories of your youth. Your voice, always so gentle and soothing. I never heard you scream, never a single foul word from your mouth; on the contrary each one was uplifting and positive. You saw the good in people and you spoke greatness into their lives. Offered a hand to anyone in need because you believed giving was truly part of loving others. Your word was as valuable as your handshake. That always impressed me. You taught me about character. You taught me all the traits that combined define a man of character, and I have lived my entire life searching for all of them in one man. And every time I'm dissapointed because the fact remains, that men like you simply don't exist anymore.

I miss your stories. You had a great talent in storytelling. As a child I looked forward to sitting on your bed, watching you rock back and forth on your rocking chair. I loved hearing about the events that shaped our countrys' history. Even more interesting with a chocolate chip cookie, you kept plenty in your room. I will always remember the story you told me, when you and grandma hid guns in the family house, you risked your life on numerous occasions. You fought for freedom in a country that was oppressed by a ruthless regime. Fought for the right for men and womento speak out against injustice, the right to choose their own path, their own god. For who is it to tell us what to believe in, who to pray to, and more importantly who to love. I admired your courage and your stories of valor have stayed with me through out the years, I wanted to be brave like you and grandma. I wanted your strength which stemmed from your kindness, and more than that I wanted to have your wisdom. You inspired me to put my faith in the same God you worshiped. I wanted the goodness you lived by to become part of me as well. I wanted to control my anger in the same way you controlled yours. And most of all, I remember you praying with me to welcome that goodness in my heart; when at twelve years old you knew it was the only thing I wanted.

After our prayer you told me how that isn't perfect, that there will be pain, but God can provide a joy that the world can't. Although, I was a child I understood your words. You also shared with me your favorite verse. Joshua 1:9 "Have I not commanded you? Be strong and courageous. Do not be afraid; do not be discouraged, for the Lord your God will be with you wherever you go." Life isn't about how you fall. Life is about being courageous and standing up. Life is about Love. Life is about the love you give without expecting a return. For how can you say you love God if you don't love your brother? I witnessed that love in you. You had a constant desire to help others. A desire that started as a child, an orphan. You were a young boy and you worked arduously for your siblings. You made sure they attended school, which in turn promised them each a brighter future. God blessed you because of it. For you were the boy who barely knew how to read and write, and you became the man who commanded the hearts of not only his family but all people he came across.

The last summer I saw your face was certainly one I won't forget, marked my life. There was a life before you and a life after you. You were falling apart. The cancer came back stronger. The entire family allowed me most your time. I only had a couple of weeks left on the island. The doctors said you only had a few months left to live. I never wanted to believe in doctors. They had said the same ten years before with your first diagnosis. I took care of you. I fed you and accompanied you to your dialysis. I held your hand in the moments you were in pain. Your mouth never uttered what I saw in your eyes. Your spark was beginning to fade and I felt it. This time around the doctors were right. I began to feel what life would be without you. Everyday I cried in private. Whose hair would I comb? Who would lift my spirits when I was down? Who would let me cry on their shoulder? You were the only one that never judged my tears. In fact you inspired me to take pride in my emotions. I wanted to remember every proverb you read to me in your angelic voice. I wanted the bottle up the feeling I felt when you would calm me with your words. I will never forget that October third morning, when we got the call you were gone. Mommy had inherited your strength. As she gasped for air to give me the news, I felt something inside of me die. I thought I was prepared to deal with your loss. I thought I was strong and courageous like you, but your death was beyond a physical one for me. It was the death of an era. Our family lost its patriarch. The month of October would never be the same.

There are times in which I feel I have fallen short, that I am not the woman you taught me to be. Yet you did always tell me it took a lot of growth, and a lot of time to become the man that I know as my grandfather, *my papacito.* I hope I am blessed with enough time to grow into the woman you envisioned me to be. Many years have passed by since you left us and I still feel you are my King David for you had his heart. You are my King Solomon for you had his wisdom. It is because of you I learned to pray for wisdom. It is because of you I watch my words. It is because of you I do things with love. You are my model for the type of person I want to be, the type of man I want my children's father to be.

The Idea Of Loving A Man Like You

I searched for you,
In every room I placed foot in.
As one who searches for a treasure.
I inhaled life every second,
I felt your eyes grace me.
As if a tiny addiction,
Was building within.
As if one look from you would suffice,
To keep a single ounce of hope alive.
Or my need to believe,
There are no coincidences
To those who believe in destiny.
In fact, I have embraced the reality,
That I am completely enamored
By the idea of loving a man like you.

All I wanted was to crush him with my words.
As if my words had the power to remove my
pain and make us even. I was wrong. My words
bounced back and cut my wound deeper. Pain is
not healed with anger. The wound only closes when
forgiveness shows its face.

Forgiveness

If someone would have told me when I met you that I was going to fall in love with you, I think I would have laughed in their face. I was young, you were only supposed to be fun, an experimental phase. But life surprised me and you were fire. A fire that consumed me, and a fire that burned me. The first to ignite a fire of anger, pity and of love. You became my creative muse in all parts of my life. Words would flow from my heart to paper, naturally. And you never knew. Ironically later you would say I was your muse.

I fell in love with your eyes from the moment we met. I wrote a hundred poems of your eyes alone. I wrote lines like such:
"You are my crude vice that I just can't quit.
The moment I feel behind me rest your eyes;
I begin to crave those pretty, pretty eyes.
I'm spellbound.
My mind loves tricking me.
In love with love
that's my attempt to kiss a lie."

They were a sweet light honey, encircled by an almond brown line, every time you looked at me there was always a spark. I'll never forget the day we met. I was so young and you were on the height of your career. I was naïve and in search for my path. It was spring in Miami, only hotter and more humid, so much so that I remembered it as summer, our summer. You stepped on the yacht, arrogant and confident. I was laying on a chair, dressed in white with a flower in my hair. Our eyes connected as you walked past me. A few steps into your walk, you turned around and smiled at me. I was hooked.

Up to then few boys had excited me enough to create those butterflies girls dream about. Immediately I felt that with you. I was certainly naïve. I didn't necessarily believe everything you told me. I was always skeptical, yet I wanted to believe in you so badly. I wanted to believe that in your eyes I was the most beautiful and sweetest girl in the world. That I was special to you. So special, that you asked me if I would marry you someday. So special, that you wanted children with me. You became a drug. You took me so high and then you would drop me so low.

The first time you dropped me low was the worse. It was almost a year into us seeing each other. I had recently moved to Los Angeles, your city. You were so excited to finally have me in your city. No longer was there resorting to hotel rooms. We were finally in your space, your bed. I loved every moment with you, and it wasn't just the sex. We would literally just lay there for hours talking, laughing, you were so charismatic and funny. A true performer in so many ways. I massaged your hands and you would play with my hair. You loved my hair, you seemed to love everything about me. So when you asked me to go on a snowboarding trip with you that January, of course I was excited. All of your friends treated me with love and respect. I felt it would be a fun trip for all of us. Little did I know it would turn into a nightmare.

It was all going great, until you made the grand mistake of sleeping with another girl in another cabin, and you thought I wouldn't find out. As I waited for you to return to our cabin, one of your friends revealed to me the truth. I couldn't believe it, I screamed at him and asked him to leave. I cried uncontrollably, struggling to catch my breath, I laid myself down until my tears ran dry and I just laid there in our bed, shocked. You were far from perfect, but the audacity. I was so confused as what to do. In a cabin, no visible roads, just snow. To think I met you under a beaming sun without a cloud in the sky, and there I was tormented in the coldest winter I had ever known. You came back to the cabin and slipped into bed as I pretended to sleep. The next day I made an excuse, a terrible headache in order to not go snowboarding. I couldn't wait for you to leave so I can continue crying. When you returned I couldn't resist but confront you. I told you I wanted to leave. When we argued I saw something in your eyes that I had never seen before, I saw anger. As your six foot plus inch frame hovered over me against the wall, all I could do was say, "I hate you". You laughed and replied "You don't hate me, you love me". And you were right, I did love you.

On my way back to LA I felt worthless. I had walked into your life a princess, and then I felt I was walking out a peasant. I stared out the window the entire ride back. I'll never forget the mountains covered in snow, and for the first time I felt my heart turn cold as ice. Any innocence that remained in me died that weekend. Of course I was hurt because you slept with someone right under my nose, but my hurt derived more from the indifference I saw in you. You were another person, someone I didn't recognize. I experienced how cruel and dishonest people can be. For months I was affected by this experience. It left some trauma in me. Years later and those mountains covered in snow still haunt me.

You would come back into my life with apologies; sadly many times I was weak for you and although I never forgot the pain you caused me, I forgave you. I have always been the stubborn type, held my share of grudges. It took a lot from me to forgive you, but something inside of me couldn't allow myself to hate you, or stay angry with you. I always felt you knew that and it gave you a certain power over me, it was true. I never knew how to say no to you. Perhaps it was my lack of experience with men that didn't allow me the bravery to quit you right away. Maybe it was a test to see how far this "bad love" would take me. Sure, it was exciting. Maybe I needed to learn about addictions, for you were one of mine. Or perhaps I felt empathy for you. I wanted to always blame your discrepancies on your difficult childhood. We played that back and forth game for two years, and even after that you felt you still had power over me. The times I told you I had a boyfriend you wouldn't respect it, in your head you always had unfinished business with me. "I don't care, it's YOU and ME. I still love you," you' would say. In our memories we were always going to have a special connection and in some dysfunctional way, I will always care for you. But you were never healthy for me. You were the knife I stabbed myself with over and over again. I will always remember our story because it was the first time I put my pride aside and forgave a man and although I was very young and didn't fully understand the power behind forgiveness, but I experienced my heart opening larger as a result. I also accepted that a man's mistakes should not reflect on how I viewed myself as a woman. In other words, I refused to walk around jaded and insecure because of your choices. I allowed myself to believe that my next love can be different. I remained positive at the idea of love finding me.

The years have passed by and we never did have that child you always asked from me. You might win "the worst boyfriend award" with many girls, but the way you love your children is a confirmation of the goodness I had seen in you. I am extremely proud of what a great father you have turned out to be. Years later I heard you had a daughter and I knew there was finally going to be a girl that was going to conquer your heart. Funny enough, she was born with your eyes, the same sweet light honey encircled by an almond brown line.

Anger, What is it?

Anger, what is it?
I know I feel it,
But do I hate it?
Is it healthy?
It is an emotion after all.
Can I quit it?
Get rid of it?
Kick it to the curb?
Like one escapes dark habits?
My only question is…*How*?
When you continue your ways with me.
Selfishly you string me along?
As if I was your puppet.
Let me remove the veil from your eyes.
You are not a ventriloquist,
And I am too heavy for strings.
I am in a desperate need
To find what anger is,
So I can show it to you,
Better yet, scream it to you,
And be freed from the desire,
To throw-
Throw objects across the room.
Hoping they never, *ever reach the wall*,
Because you stand
Between the wall and I.
I wish I did not fear,
I rather wish I was a coward,
To say and do all these things,
Then later blame it on my Anger.

I Am His Prey

Teach me how to quit him.
How to free my thoughts of him?
I have tried fighting it,
But he keeps taking control of me.
Like a moth to a fire,
He always consumes me.
Our differences are our only common ground,
And silence has always been our stance.
Still, Passion exists.
When our eyes meet,
When his breath becomes mine,
And mine becomes his.
If this is love,
Cruel should be its name.
Only cruelty stabs the heart,
Then slowly pulls away.
Viciously, Selfishly,
And still,
I am his prey.

Maktub

Love me as I love you.
Not with ego,
But with heart, mind, and soul.
Let my scent become your addiction,
And my eyes become your windows.
Dream of me,
I'll be your muse.
Out of the waters,
This Naiad was born to please you.
Let my face be a constant glare,
And my body your haunting shadow.
Let my smile give you peace of mind,
While my lips bring you life.
Let our history become a story,
Of love transcending every barrier.
Sands and sea,
Won't come between us,
Our fates collided for a reason.
Never dubious, never intimidated,
Because our story…it was written.

Pieces

When I see your name,
I see love.
Yet, when I hear it,
I feel torture.
Unrequited Love,
The passionate poet named it.
The feeling of desperation,
That drowns you in isolation.
Loving from a distance,
Can break a heart in an instant,
But if life permits it,
Destined I was to live it.
If that's the price I have to pay,
Let my heart then,
Shatter into pieces.
One truth be told,
That each tiny piece,
Is entwined with my soul,
And each piece,
Will love you more
Than my heart,
As a whole.

Checkmate

You are my seduction,
Mixed with passion and kissed with desire.
My love for you will never be lost,
Only hidden within shadows.
I am not her,
She is not me.
Therefore, we both don't fit in.
Simply another story lived.
Destiny plays games,
But King and Queen in chess,
Never together stay.
So a promenade I take.
While in your throne you rest,
With your pawns, knights, and rooks you shall remain.
This queen deserves an official reign,
No longer we shall mate,
Only reminisce in the memories the ocean raised.

Promises

I promised to never cry a single tear for you again.
I promised to never write about your eyes again.
In the past is where your smile belongs.
Yet, today I asked myself:
Can promises be broken?
And mistakes be drowned,
In anything else but sorrows?
Because the fact remains,
That you are the inspiration,
That consumes my thoughts,
And without you my muse is dry.
I tried shutting down the dam of tears,
But it's useless, it breaks.
At the mere idea of having lost you forever.
My throat is made of knots,
The ache has gone beyond my heart,
And reached my soul.

You Are That Man!

I say it's over,
But how do I say goodbye?
When you are the man that I love,
And can't live without.

You are that man that stops my world.
That quiets every noise around me.
That makes me stand still in time,
And cherish each moment,
Spent by your side.

You are that man that stole my heart,
And soul combined.
You are my pleasure and my pain.
The one who holds the balance,
to my scale.

You are that man that inspires in me,
Love and hate.
For you are the source of my extremities.
You live in my conscious and subconscious,
Because you are that man I can't forget.

You are that man that turns me inside out,
And makes me weak to my disdain.
You simply are that love I was meant to live,
Even if in the end,
Fate didn't choose me.

Goddess in the Sunrise

Countless are the days,
In which the sun has set and risen.
I held on to the air between us,
To the last breath exchanged,
To the last laugh we shared.
Many moons have come and gone,
While the stars fed me hope,
Giving me dreams,
That only Aphrodite knows.
Yet, in the morning the sun always rose,
The sound of the lyre never did I hear,
Apollo always brought reality to my ear.
The wind the truth did gently whisper,
But blind was my love,
And my heart stubborn as a goat.
In numerous occasions to the wind I replied:

> My lover's eyes are like the sun,
>
> My love for him is always young,
>
> Rain is he to my drought,
>
> Destiny to me he brought.

For years I cried rivers of broken ego,
I was slowly becoming Hera, a jealous sap.
A fool was I to believe in his empty smile,
The strength to dismiss him from my life,
Never did I try to find.

Always running back to his pretty eyes.
Until today Athena's wisdom my soul revived,
The song of morning birds,
Awoke my sleeping pride,
And resuscitated the goddess that lived inside.

I write about love.
I feel as if I have studied love.
The one love that never ceases to impress me is the
love God has for me.
For I have cheated on him, and he always takes me
back, and when I fall,
there he is to help me rise.
He is my protector, my savior, my provider,
my healer, my friend, my king,
and my father.
He is perfection combined.
The only competition any man in my life
will ever have.

Knowledge

I am entirely your daughter but parts of me always yearned to be your friend. It is said that the relationship a woman has with her father determines the relationship she will have with her spouse. If that holds true then my relationship will have respect. Even with your shortcomings, all my life I truly respected you and admired you. Daddy, I have always thought you were the most talented, most intelligent man I have ever known. Your knowledge in the arts still impresses me. The way your fingers maneuver a keyboard, or the strings of a guitar, a beautiful thing to see. When we speak about literature your memory always exceeds my expectations. You always finish your verses when you begin to recite them. You seemed to already know all the answers to all my questions about everything I wanted to know. I was terrible at mathematics and at one point you were a math teacher. I wasn't the smartest in science, but somehow with you I understood physics. There is no one better in my book, to discuss theology and the bible than you. Even in your traditional way of thinking you always found a way to infuse the arts. But it was more than knowledge I wanted from you, I wanted a certain intimacy, one that would help me confide in you.

I was twenty-three years old and had gotten in trouble. I was trying to defend a friend and it left me in an emergency room with a bloody head injury. There are girls in this world that would have called their Daddy first, I was only trying to figure out how I would hide this from you. I have lived my life hiding things from you. It wasn't easy growing up with you expecting so much from me. How could you expect for me to be a porcelain doll, when you weren't perfect? I was not a little girl anymore. By then I had done many things you had dictated I could never do. I had already had sex out of wedlock, drank alcohol and partied in extravagant places. God knows I drove drunk too many times and was always walking a slippery line. I knew I wanted to be a great woman but I was so caught up in living a decadent life. Of course I had my restraints, in the end the seed you and Mom planted in me was stronger than most desires. I wasn't a slut and I never touched drugs. And nonetheless, there I was in a Los Angeles hospital injured and feeling alone while you were two thousand miles away without the slightest idea of what was happening to your little girl.

A few days later you found out about the incident and my injury. You screamed at me and told me it was my fault. I asked, how in God's green earth is helping a friend in a dangerous situation my fault, you replied "18 Inches!" I knew I had a severe head injury but I genuinely did not understand what you meant. So you made a point, "Do you know that every decision in your life is based on 18 inches?" I still didn't understand. *"Put your hand on your heart, then walk it to your brain. That's 18 inches baby. Scientifically the average distance between the heart and the brain is 18 inches, and you have to learn the difference. To succeed you must make decisions with your brain. When you think with your heart, you are making emotional decisions. I know you want to succeed, so you HAVE to learn the difference! Do you understand?"* Like most average parents, you never knew how to give me advice. It's not your fault, no one ever taught you. So when you did give me advice it was as if I were one of your students. As if I could learn about life through a textbook. But that day your "18 inches" analogy marked me, you were right. Up to then I had lived my life only thinking with my heart. I was passionate about everything I did. I actually only did things if my heart was in it. Maybe you expected so much from me because you saw part of you in me. Maybe your heart also drove you, and that was the cause of some failures in your life that impacted our family. Maybe you screaming at me was a release of your frustrations, not wanting me to go down the same road. Daddy, maybe I haven't vocalized it enough, maybe I don't call you enough, but I want to thank you for loving me and teaching me about the power of decisions, for all the knowledge you have passed on to me, I'll always be grateful for that. I'll always love you more than words can express, and more than science can ever make sense.

To Dream In English

Leaving one's country
Is like the yanking of a plant,
With the humid soil,
Alive in its root.

Leaving one's country
Is like an open bloody wound.

I cannot remember
The calm breeze of your winter,
Nor how the flamboyant,
Blooms in the spring.

All I have left of you,
Are the illusions,
Of what our lives,
In synchronized motion could have been.

They chose a dream,
They chose a dream for me.

To dream in English,
Is what they did.
Sacrificed the beat of their hearts,
For Yankee Possibilities.

Now many full moons,
Have graced the sky,
Wishing they can turn back time,
To relive the drums of their Caribbean past.

Salt in their tears,
Like the Salt of the Ocean that seasoned their lives.

Not I, My soul won't ever say goodbye.
That land I will forever,
Have imprinted in my heart,
All with immense pride.

I don't believe in regrets,
but I'm haunted tragically by the day
I lied to you and told you I did not love you
anymore.

Change

    I kissed you over and over. I kissed you everywhere. Actually, except your toes, I think. I caressed each pore of your body. I stared into your eyes on numerous occasions. I've seen honesty in your eyes. I laughed with you. Danced. You made me to smile. I spoke to you in every language I know. I hugged you so hard, while kissing each light freckle on your back. I played with your soft curls and made fun of your laugh. I listened to you. I heard you talk about what you loved and the man you wished to become. I took care of you when you were sick. We developed a bond. Still, it didn't matter what I did and what I felt we shared. You were not yet a prince, but still a frog.

    When we first met I knew I wasn't ready for a relationship, my heart had just been shattered a few months before. I've come to understand that every person comes into our lives for a specific reason, and for a specific season, and it was destiny for us to meet. You didn't teach me about philosophy nor did I find religion through you. You didn't teach me about art nor science. You didn't teach me about sports nor anything in particular, but you inspired change in me. Because if you were still a frog I must admit I was still a fly. During that time I seemed to be extremely concerned about all the wrong things. It was the typical situation of a girl stuck in a certain way of thinking, in which prioritized all the vanities of life. Yes, I was a kind and truthful person, I cared about others and had a desire to please God; but when it came to the opposite sex, I had it all wrong. I gave more importance to nourishing the physical over the spiritual. Physical attributes or the chemistry under the sheets does not keep the man. A woman is beyond the physical. A woman is beyond the clothes she wears, beyond her makeup or perfect hair. Of course a woman should always take care of herself but in the end those things can change at any given moment. The core of who you are as a person is what remains. A woman's heart should serve as an example to her family and the world.

At times I was immature, sometimes I acted out of spite. I listened to my friends more than I listened to my heart. I tested your trust, you tested mine, and after two years of playing the game we played so well, we had a conversation that changed everything. You sat across from me in your loft and asked me if I wanted to get married. I don't think you were specifically asking me to marry you right there and then, but more or so you wanted to know where my mindset was. I responded honestly and said "someday." It's interesting to think that at the same age my mother had already birthed me and had a four year old. Marriage was the last thing on my mind. Of course I loved you and was ready to take the relationship more seriously. At that point I would have done many things for you but I still had a wall that I had built after experiencing previous disillusionments. I felt that becoming an independent woman was to not depend on any man, except maybe my father. How can I contemplate marriage with a man, and not completely trust men with personal situations and feelings of mine? The truth is I never envisioned marriage with you but I still wanted you. And although you never taught me anything unforgettable you always gave me a certain passion. Always the most perfect kiss, the perfect touch, and it was inconceivable for me to live my life without that.

The following months after that definitive conversation, I missed you terribly. I missed you to the point I had insomnia filled nights. I didn't know how to rip you out of my heart, because the truth is I cared for you more than my pride would ever allow me to admit. Still even in the midst of missing you as I did, I was selfish and could not see my contribution into why we failed. I only saw you and "your ways" and all the reasons you were still a frog. I wanted to place all the blame on you and your womanizing traits. You had your demons. I had mine too. I failed to see that a real woman speaks to the king in the frog. A real man speaks to the queen in the fly. And we never did that for each other. We attacked each other, focused on our weaknesses, but didn't make each other necessarily better. We were selfish and love isn't selfish, love is meant to be self-less. I understood that I had lost you. I couldn't turn back the hands of time and dissolve the mistakes I made with you. I couldn't take back the terrible things I said. Words are powerful and I hurt you with them. I couldn't take back the disrespect. You couldn't turn back the hands of time and be a better man, because what was done was done. Nonetheless something stirred my insides, my way of thinking and my way of loving. I began to soul search and I began to realize my mistakes and I vowed to be a different girl for the next man in my life. I decided to walk the line. I chose to become more of an example. I chose to nurture my spirit and my gifts. I chose to awake the goddess that lived in me. Because why would a girl want to be treated like a princess or a woman want to be treated like a queen? When there is a rare species that prefers to be treated as a myth. For why would I want to be a mere mortal if there is a *Goddess* that lives in me? I realized the immense potential of the woman in me, and I made a choice to become her, the woman I yearned to be.

I Want More

I don't wish upon stars,
I know they are too far.
My soul seeks answers,
For what can't be touched,
Just felt beneath it all.
All and everything that consumes my existence,
Yet I can't explain-
The desire of wanting clarity,
Without it driving me to insanity.
I ask- *is this all in vain?*
Can this red wine taste like heaven?
Can it fill the void of my empty lips on this shattered night?
If you possess the power,
To arouse me with a kiss,
Can you provide me inner peace?
You can always release my oxytocins,
But in the end,
A little pleasure doesn't heal my pain,
Even if that's your only aim.
The truth is that my pleasure is not your aim- *I know.*
Satisfaction of your ego
And your male libido,
That I know is your aim.
Comprehend that tying me down in the physical,
Can cause some tingles,
Even make my spine quickly shiver,
But it won't grasp,
Nor surprise my inner spiritual.
Just remember,
I might laugh and moan,
And adore the things you do with your tongue,
But that isn't love...

I want more.

The Night and Her Half-Moon

Tonight half a moon stares above the city,
That became an accomplice in our story.
The same half-moon
That would often coyly peak through the window,
The nights you chose to love me.
Tonight I notice her,
Just how I noticed her last night,
And the night before.
Ever since this world turned quiet without you.
Quiet in the midst of champagne and laughter.
Quiet in a pool of empty kisses and temporary pleasures.
Like the moon I am full of deep craters,
All result of the impact your silence has left in me.
A silence that I can't break,
But I try to forget with each toast,
Fake embrace,
And with every scratch of the turntables
That gives life to the decadence,
That only the night provides.
In the end it all remains the same.
You and your unshaken silence.
The quiet night,
With the same half-moon,
Like the one that coyly peaked,
On those nights you chose to love me.

We Don't Hold Hands...

The man I hang with,
We don't hold hands,
I allow him
To touch every single pore of my body,
I let him penetrate me physically and mentally,
And I still don't hold his hand?
My mother would be ashamed
To say she raised me.
Where is the poise?
Where is my self-respect when I need it the most?

He enters me,
Seductively he whispers,
That my pussy is his.
How dare he think my pussy is his?
He hasn't bought it!
God knows I haven't seen a single penny
Invested in my pussy!
But I remain quiet,
Not wanting to ruin
The *so-called* moment.
Why disrupt the one thing he's good at?
Orgasms- giving and receiving them.
In true altruistic fashion.
Because if fucking was an art,
He can paint masterpieces all day long.
And he sure has mastered his brush strokes.
The impressionists would be jealous,
Of how smooth he strokes my canvas.
Including Renoir in all his glory.

Except that Classics are hard to beat,
And sadly he's everything but a classic.

So, why do I let him?
Touch me, tease me, please me?
Have control of my utmost single weakness?
Because I love him?
Look how far love has gotten me...
We don't even hold hands in public.

V-Tonic

It's all a blur,
How I shook you out of my life.
The Russians got it right,
With the vodka this time.
A girl can say some hurtful things,
When the liquor percentage goes sky high.
Tell me,
What else was I supposed to do?
Than take another swig,
Of that v-tonic with the lime on the rocks.
You blatantly held her hand,
How dare you kiss her in my presence?
It's okay....
She lacks my lips and my essence.
So what if I'm a flirt,
I'm a good girl at heart.
Insecure men like you,
Can make any good girl go bad,
And say, "fuck the world" at times.
I won't succumb like that,
I won't let you win like that,
I'm too good for that.
Stay with your average chick,
I'm sure you'll mold her right.
I do admit you caught me off guard,
You were my love toy,
You sure turned on me,
And played me right back.

I Was She, Before Becoming Me

She chased the type of love
That was like a summer wind.
It made her feel alive
In the midst of heat,
As if it was necessary for her to live.
Sadly, no one told her
It was impossible to catch and keep,
Things that are volatile,
Like a fleeting wind.

LETTER VII

Never fear someone for their abilities,
fear them for their purpose.

Perseverance

Not many people are blessed enough to say they were born with raw distinct talent, and you have that privilege. Maybe you inherited all of Daddy's talents and some of Mom's too. Perhaps, even of an uncle or two as well. That's how incredibly talented you are and always have been. Since we were children you had an innate power to make people laugh and to make them feel. To the point you drove some people insane. I remember the first time I realized you had a calling for music. You were five years old. You played with all of Daddy's instruments and went everywhere with your drumsticks. It was so amazingly annoying. One Christmas morning you received the gift you wanted for months, your very own set of drums. You were ecstatic! Your big hazel eyes opened wide, and you couldn't wait to start playing. *You sure played, and you didn't stop playing!* Every morning from the minute you woke until you went to sleep. You were persistent with the drums. Our sister and I would implore for you to take a break. We already had the loudest household in the neighborhood. Daddy always had one or two TV's on and simultaneously played his instruments. I felt I lived in a house full of crazies.

One day I cracked open your room door. Of course, you didn't notice me because you were enchanted by the sounds you were creating. You were entranced as I watched you and felt extremely proud. Although, the noise bothered me most of the time, I knew I was witnessing something special. You continued to impress me many times because you were always so witty and original.

Fast forward years later we were talking on the phone and you expressed to me how you decided to pursue your dreams as a musician because of me. You said that when I moved to Los Angeles to pursue my dreams in the entertainment industry without knowing anyone, I inspired you. When we were kids you always thought I was better than who I was. You always saw greatness in me. You believed in me. I had no choice but to persevere. Sometimes all we need in life is someone who believes in us. I truly believe that every person who has achieved personal or professional greatness had someone who motivated him or her to reach their goals. I was lucky to have had people motivate me during difficult times, but that day your words impacted me. I felt I had a duty as your older sister to continue on setting an example of strength and of perseverance, because I understood my example encouraged you more than any advice I could give you. When things were difficult and I struggled to survive in a new city, I constantly thought about how I couldn't let you down. I knew my reaction to my own obstacles would influence how you would react if you experienced similar obstacles. I understood I had to instill in you the same belief I had, one of never giving up until seeing our destiny fulfilled.

I Fight

Fighting with walls is all I have ever done.

I fight, I fight.

They will topple someday.
Everything breaks, *that I know.*

I fight, I fight.

These walls will break.
No storm lasts forever, *that I know.*

I will fight until my destiny prevails someday.
I will fight until my strength ceases no more.
I will fight until I see these walls break.

The Secret

Love...
That's how the weak
Are destroyed.
They meet someone stronger,
Who doesn't love them enough.

If only I can feed you pills
And give you eyes
For your soul.
To provide a cure
for your own demise.

If only I can teach you,
It is all in the mind.
The weak are actually strong,
For they have endured pain
And survived.

If only I can teach you,
The difference between
The strong and the weak.
I will whisper the secret,
softly yet clear...

The strong paint smiles on,
And give thanks for their pain.
While the weak live in tears,
In pity and shame.

I'm Zealous Of My Pain

I like pain.
No I'm not a masochist.
I like pain, because it's necessary for growth.
I've gotten to know parts of me,
I didn't know existed.
I have felt things that only my tears know.
With those tears I have liberated myself,
From hurt, shame and fears.
I have become a real woman through pain.
So yes,
I need pain.
About the same way I need love.
My soul has become more beautiful through pain.
I'm zealous of my pain.

*A woman's heart shouldn't be judged by the
amount of times it has been broken,
but more for its strength to know
when to walk away.*

Failure

Being in sync with the one you love has to be one
of the most beautiful feelings a human being can ever
experience. I think back to certain moments in my life in
which I felt nothing else in the world existed but him and
I. An incredible happiness overtakes you and you can't help
but smile. This feeling you yearn to relive everyday. Then the
day comes you realize just how rare those moments are; and
you learn that sadly those same extraordinary moments can
become plagued with pain.

It seems that during our three-year relationship all I
did was forgive you. I loved you ardently and I forgave you,
because any time there was a rift you made me feel we couldn't
be apart. Maybe it was simply masochism veiled as love. For
whatever the reason I needed you. I loved making love to
you, particularly after a fight. I loved the way you would
tell me you loved me when you were inside of me. Making
love to you was unlike any of the other men before you. In
addition to all the passion lovemaking with you was spiritual.
A spiritual connection mixed with pain. It was wanting to
spend the rest of my life with you and knowing you wouldn't
be mine forever. The comfort of living with you, and waking
up next to you everyday still never provided me peace. You
would never be satisfied, and we would eventually end. You

were always going to want it all, and that all included other women. I'll never understand how you could love me and still lust for others. It's what made us different. I loved to a point of no return and you were still learning what love was.

Of course we had problems. Everything that lives encounters problems. But you stabbed my heart when your empty eyes looked at me and said that love was not enough. I was speechless, to me love was everything. In my life love was you and love was us. Was it not enough? There were times I was convinced you loved me desperately. Convinced you needed me. But to need someone is a dangerous, particularly for a man. At first it is great because you realize you have grown to love your other half, you trust them with everything. I know you trusted me with anything. You trusted me with your fears. You trusted me with your desires, with your work, and your life. We were so in sync, you were my best friend. We were consumed by each other. Needing me eventually became your crutch. A man needs to feel like a man, when he finds himself depending on a woman he can begin to feel emasculated. I did that to you, I did that to *us*. My only desire was to help you become better, for you to be the man that I felt was hidden inside of you. I failed to understand perhaps you weren't ready to be the type of man I was seeking. It didn't matter how much I tried to make you happy, to make us happy, I was continuously going to fail; it was as if your intention was never to win with me. I failed, I should have accepted you for you, instead of trying to make you into a better you. Although you must admit that my motivation translated into a more successful "you". But you needed to find your "better" on your own, without me advising you on what to do. But how can you love someone the way I loved you and let them take the wrong turns, down wrong roads? With you I learned that a man is like the trunk of a tree. Winds will blow, storms will pour, and like a child one can carve their initials and still the trunk will stand. Change can only exist if by the root you pull, but to rip its soul from the soil should remain God's work anyways.

After our breakup you expressed with frustration that you and I could never be anything else if we weren't together. That was difficult for me to hear, considering you were my best friend. The notion of being strangers shocked me and hurt me. For who was I going to share all the details of my day with? Who was going to listen to me ramble on about my ideas? Who was going to challenge my mind? Who was I going to watch movies with? Who was going to download all of the new music for me? Who was going to remember to put my water on my nightstand before bed? Who was going to move my hair from my face while I slept? Dry me after my night sweats? Give me my vitamins? Who was going to bother me about eating more? Who would remind me two drinks was enough? Because the same way I felt I had taken care of you, you took care of me.

Part of me wanted to ask you to stay. To stay and fight for me, to fight for us. But a certain ideology impeded me from doing so. The idea that when someone loves you enough, you won't have to ask, they will stay on their own. The inevitable occurred, and there I stood alone in what used to be our bedroom and cried. I cried silently, knowing that if those walls could have consoled me they would have. I was a helpless child mourning the death of everything you were in my life. The death of my friend, my lover, my partner, the father of the child we never had. A sense of loneliness enveloped me, when I realized that perhaps you were right. Maybe you and I could never be anything else other than together. For we had reached a deep, intense level of love and stories like ours sometimes just end without proper goodbyes. Stories like ours are lived and left to dry with unanswered questions, all because we both had too much pride.

We became strangers, exactly what I feared. You went on with your life and seemed not to be affected by the loss of me. I know I appeared to have moved on fast, but there wasn't a day I did not think of you. There wasn't a day I didn't feel the ghost of you lingering around me. I still slept on my side of the bed, I still kept the blinds open just how you liked it. I thought of you when I would light our candles, and when I would make our bed. You were always better at setting the sheets than me. All the times I wanted to tear our pictures or delete them I never could. Although some people can't be anything else other than together, I had to keep some part of you. Even with feelings of anger, loss and failure I understood that erasing you from my memories meant losing the girl I was when I was with you. And although I'm not that girl anymore, I want to remember her. I want to remember her spark and the smile that you brought out in me. The same way I want to remember the man you were, the man I knew, the man I loved so deeply.

A Lover's Death

You are gone.
Forever,
We said goodbye.
But sometimes when the sun sets,
The ghost of you,
Trickles and circles this room.
Sometimes I smile,
And sometimes my eyes fill with water.
Deaths occur,
And lovers part,
But through it all,
Memories seem to live,
And haunt with immortal pride.

I Decided To Baptize Our Bed

I decided to baptize our bed,
With another man's scent.
A rebirth, free from your aura.
I'm going to roll around
And make lust on our Egyptian linen.
Then I will shred them to pieces.
For I have decided to baptize our bed,
With another man's scent.
Hopefully his aroma proves strong enough
To clean what's left of your energy.
Out of this house, out of this room.
Most importantly out of my flesh,
That still craves parts of you.

There, I Still Will Be

I gave you the sun
But you wanted the moon.
When I gave you the moon,
You wanted the stars.
So I reached blindly,
For the most infinite stars,
And wrapped myself
Around each one of them,
Just for you.
The stars, the moon and the sun combined,
Weren't enough for your fickle heart.
So I took my tears,
And made you a sea,
So you can sail the earth
And find the impossible treasure,
You constantly seek.
Yet every morning,
My sun will be there to wake you.
Every night,
My moon will be there to calm you.
And if you ever need me,
Look amongst the stars,
Wrapped in each one of them,
There, I still will be.

The Angel

His distinct natural smell.
I loved to smell the soap off his bare chest.
The way our minds synced,
Only we understood each other.
We lived a dream within a dream,
Sometimes painful
But sometimes full of desire.
We moved together,
As two people who only had each other.
And we loved each other in moments
We will never have again.
Because love can be great
But king and queen in chess never together stay.
One must die as sacrifice for the other.
Although my love for him was the greatest I ever felt,
I refused to die just yet,
I chose to keep on living.
To him a ghost I might remain,
But in my heart I'll be an angel
Who will forever guard his steps.

Who Was I?

I fell in love with the complexity
Of your mind,
The way our thoughts
Would often collide,
Who was I to change you?
I saw your wounds still open,
My only desire was to sew them,
Who was I to fix you?
I saw you broken on the ground,
I used my strength to make you whole
Who was I to lift you?
You felt lost,
And when I found you,
Who was I to think my love could keep you?

I Will Always Love You

My favorite part of loving you,
Was always when I hugged you.
As if a hug from me can fix your childhood.
As if a hug from me can protect you from yourself
And your fears.
As if a hug from me,
Can mend all of your broken pieces.
Because at the end of the day,
No one understands you the way I do.
No one knows you the way I do.
For I know every side of you,
Every good,
Every flaw,
All the things that you desire,
All the things that can destroy you,
That's our bond.
Here I am,
My love hasn't flickered,
I will always love you.

My heart tried to put you aside,
Like one who glues paper over paint.
Useless for the paper always crumbles,
The air always cracks the paper-thin.
Meanwhile the paint underneath
remains the same.
Just remember,
My facade has been the paper,
And you forever are my solemn paint.

Resentment

I still remember the morning years ago I realized I had fallen in love with you. I awoke and there you were, on the pillow next to mine again. I had already become used to your scent. My body belonged in your bed. I looked at you and understood I was experiencing a different type of love. This time around it wasn't based on lust, it wasn't selfish; it was a love I felt proud about. A love that made me feel purely human. A sense of peace enveloped me. I wanted to learn every motion you made during your sleep. Every pore of your skin, curvature of your lips, and suddenly I embraced you. I desired for you to feel what I was feeling, through my arms, I hoped it was contagious. Little did I know that day I was about to embark on an enormous life lesson. A lesson that only time had the power of healing. Even still I feel the texture of the scars this lesson left in me. In the cracks between the scars there is gratitude. Gratitude for the woman I have become. A strength I discovered during my nights of solitude. The strength and beauty I believe is only found in pain.

Does too much familiarity kill love? Does it drain the senses? Can seeing your lover all day, every day, destroy the passion? Is there no excitement in the "little" things anymore because you've gotten used to them? You know what he's going to say before he opens his mouth. You know his reactions when someone walks past, or makes an absurd comment. You know which side he always sleeps, and what time he likes to wake. You know exactly how he likes every meal prepared. You know the things he can't live without. You know every product he uses, how he wears his clothes, what seasons he prefers, and what mood he likes you best in. Then one day you wake up and your love is drowning in tears. The love that you felt was strong enough to survive an apocalypse was barely hanging on. The love you felt you could never live without was slipping through life's cracks; those separate moments in which trust is tested. You begin to wonder what you're doing wrong.

Do you remember telling me you'll never let me go? Do you remember all the potential I saw in you? Do you remember telling me "We'll always fix any problem"? Do you remember telling me I was the woman you had loved the most? Do you remember telling me you hoped for me to remain in your life in good times, the same way I had remained through the difficult times? Do you remember all the times you told me you were ready? Do you remember telling me I was your home? Do you remember talking about the next years by my side? Do you remember the nights I consoled you, promised you I'd never leave you? Do you remember me taking care of you? Making breakfast, lunch, and dinner. I did your laundry, as it was a job. Do you remember me helping build your business? Do you remember the sleepless nights I spent with you writing and conceptualizing a business plan? Do you remember how I spent more of my time building your career than my own? Do you remember how you would refer to us as "WE" before it turned into "ME"? Do you remember how I used every contact I had in order to help you get your company off the ground? I used my social skills to build you up because you weren't much of a social being. I knew about your deeply rooted insecurities that you attempted to cover up with a gang of tattoos. You have drifted through life as a gypsy seeking love to replace a certain emptiness. Unknowingly making every woman that has loved you pay for how your mother made you feel. I knew your pain and because I knew the effect that pain caused you, I chose and vowed to love you differently than I had ever loved any man. I chose to love you unconditionally.

Once you tasted a tiny bit of success you forgot everything I once meant to you, and everything we were building. I had no choice but to do what I had promised to never do. I let you go. In the quest to make you happy, I made the mistake so many women in love make, I forgot to love myself first, and grew unhappy. I knew that it didn't matter how great of a woman I was or how loyal and supportive of a partner I could be, you were selfish. I made the decision to return back to me. To love myself and revive the essence in me that your lack of appreciation had dimmed. I no longer wanted to sneak out the bedroom, go into the bathroom and cry in the middle of the night. Yes, that's what I did, I didn't want you to see me cry. I know there were times you noticed. I didn't want to hurt you so I made up excuses. That's how pure my love was. I was hurting and I still cared more for your feelings than my own.

When we parted my mind raced at all our unanswered questions. Questions I attempted to answer with your actions because they certainly spoke louder than your words. Perhaps, you think you hurt me with your words. Those words that only a cold man could say. Certain days, I thought you only said those horrible things out of frustration. The frustration of knowing you lost me forever. Admitting to yourself you hurt the woman who loved you during a time in which you didn't even love yourself. Is it possible that in your complex mind you created the notion that I abandoned you?

I remember the day you finished moving your things out, we shared an elevator ride downstairs and you compared my doings to your mother's mistakes. I asked myself why you said such a terrible thing. I was letting you go, for you to find your way. You had an urge to explore things you hadn't lived and women you hadn't slept with. I refused to chase you. I let you go with the hope you would find yourself back to me, back into the arms of the woman who loved you genuinely from the start. The stars aligned themselves elsewhere, in a way I didn't expect. They aligned themselves opposite of you. You damaged us, and there was no longer a visible road to you.

This Must Be Love

In my world love has come and gone,
And with every failure I found myself asking what love was.
This morning, the raindrops that brushed against the steel
That shapes your bedroom windows,
Gave clue to what love could be.
The soothing sounds of God's tears woke me,
And the calmness of having your warmth next to me
 left me still.
For I had to forever remember the exact moment.,
In which my eyes opened large
At the realization that once again
Your head lay on the pillow next to mine.
I once again was embraced
By the comfort of your perfect body,
As my lips once again,
Were attracted to the smoothness of your back.
In that moment a certain peace enveloped me,
And I softly murmured to myself:
This must be love.
All while you innocently enjoyed your sleep,
All while I innocently pulled you, closer to me.

A Sorry Is Not Enough

Can a sorry glue back glass,
After being shattered into pieces?
Can a sorry repair a car,
After being crashed without remorse?
Can a sorry mend a bond,
After it's been shredded to its final cord?
How I would love
For a simple sorry
To be the answer for all the resentment,
I have shamefully held inside.
Unfortunately,
My heart is stubborn
And my scars remind me,
How a sorry is simply,
Not enough.

Beating Hearts

These hearts aren't beating together,
Nor do they cry together,
Not anymore.
The time in which I sensed
Each of your sensibilities,
Reciprocated by your devilish smile,
Those years have expired.
Expired like the milk that we were.
When all I yearned was for us to be wine.
Sweet Red Wine.
How I would have loved to crush grapes,
In the middle of summer with you.
Instead we crushed dreams.
My dreams.

Emotions

I swim in a river of emotions.
Its water has turned my hot heart cold.
Its rocks and branches,
Are harsh like the words,
You left imprinted in my mind.
This river has overflowed,
With heavy emotions.
Torrents of love.
Torrents of hate.
For it is true
What lovers and warriors say.
There is a thin line,
Between love and hate.
And I swift from hating you,
To loving you,
To hating you all over again.

Obsolete

Our story is like a metal that oxidized,
And the rustiness can cut
Dangerously deep.
I sent you to the abyss of my thoughts.
An abyss where only
The purest of darkness lives.
Sadly one where love can't bear,
But surrender and simply not exist.
As memories soon become obsolete,
It is obvious you and I will never be,
Anything close to what we were,
And everything we could have been.

Our Bed

Nostalgic at the ghostly memories
That lay on this bed.
I remember when you purchased it.
When we laid on it for the first time.
When our feet embraced,
Getting to know the tickle
And cold that only pre-mature love knows.
The years of comfort we built,
The amazing conversations we had,
The fights that boiled when passion collides,
The early routines that rose from too much familiarity,
The ideas we dreamt,
The love we made,
The love that burned away.
Now I face our bed,
Our Egyptian cotton Sheets
Stare at me asking where your hands went.
I stand numb and confused,
At the once inconceivable task
Of making this bed alone.

The Knot Of You

There is this tension that has built
In the center of my chest.
It feels as if a knot sits there unmoved,
And my breath asks for its permission to go around it.
Simply to breathe.
I paint smiles on,
Laughs will escape my mouth at times.
And when I forget the knot exists,
A small sharp pain occurs,
To remind me it is still very present in me.
And I live my life like this.
Watching the days turn into months,
As I fight to continue breathing,
With the knot that never dissolves.
That knot is you.
What I would do to breathe freely again,
Without carrying the knot of you inside of me.

Liar

He doesn't realize that every time he lies,
He's committing suicide in front of me.
He's killing everything I see in him.
If only he could honest be,
Because God knows I hate to watch him bleed.

When I Loved You

When I loved you,
It was like ice skating on a rink.
I skated freely,
Until the ice cracked on the brink.

That's when I learned
About numbness,
When my heart turned cold,
And fell into darkness.

For how can love blink,
Without brightness,
When I loved you,
With a love that was pride-less.

So I drifted away with the cracked ice,
Said goodbye to those cold nights.
Gambled with your black lies,
While you lost with your dud dice.

For I am that woman,
You'll never gain back,
But maybe someday,
You will play right.

Say You Will

Will you miss me
when I'm gone?

Lie if you must.

But please,
say you will.

And the Echo
of your voice
will suffice.

I can stand next to you,
Close enough to feel your breath
Embrace the deepest pore of my skin,
And I can still look you in the eyes
and lie.
Lie for example,
That what you did to my heart,
Doesn't matter anymore.
Lie and whisper in your ear,
I'm not hurt anymore.
Lie and scream from the top of my lungs,
That I don't care anymore.
Lie and walk away after telling you,
I don't love you anymore.

Shame

You humiliated me publicly out of spite, you told me you wanted to make me feel how I had made you feel. I read those words over a hundred times. I couldn't understand what you meant, all I did was live to make you better. I was devoted day after day to see you happy. Such a difficult task because you embodied sadness from early from the start. I once read in a book that a man will never be truly happy until he feels accomplished, until he feels he can provide. Although you had immense potential, I knew you weren't in that place in your life yet. You had the desire to succeed and I made the choice to support you in the process. I was your emotional support. Many times you expressed how much you hated your life and contemplated quitting. I don't think you can comprehend how much it drained me. I wasn't myself anymore. I no longer was the positive and energetic girl you first met. The girl you were attracted to and supposedly fell in love with. I became a reflection of you. I became negative. I became depressed. I became all the traits I tried so hard to help you overcome. Shamefully, I became someone I did not want to be. While you on the other hand, took my light. I had no guilt for initiating our demise. The only guilt, the realization that maybe I should have let you go long before I did.

There is no worst feeling than being used by the person you love. At first I didn't want to admit it, part of me felt you had loved me very much. As the months progressed after we parted ways, and after conversations I had with people that knew us, it became evident you indeed used me. Perhaps you never calculated it, but you knowingly took advantage of me. When this realization occurred I became ashamed of what we had once shared, ashamed for having vouched for you. Ashamed for trusting you with all of me. You were the only man who had seen me cry. The only man I had trust with my fears and failures. My shame was so strong that I avoided certain people and certain places. All because I feared thevquestions that would arise in regards to our broken relationship. How could I look at friends and acquaintances and admit they were right about your true colors, that I had been blind for all those years.

I did what many people do in an anxious mental state, escaped the only way I knew how: I went out to countless dinners, bars and clubs, I went on meaningless dates, became cynical about love. I started to have selfish thoughts. I traveled outside of my comfort zone. Some nights I became excessively drunk. Sometimes those nights were my favorite, the nights in which I forgot your name. I felt what it was like to be free again. Unfortunately that freedom was only temporary, I would wake and find my heart still bleeding for you.

I knew I needed to heal myself from within. I couldn't cry for you anymore when you didn't deserve my tears. Of course time heals the wound, but even with the lack of tears my spirit still ached from the resentment. It's as if all the love I once had for you had turned to hate. This hate weighed me down and I knew it wasn't who I was. I wasn't the kind of woman who hated others. I was the kind of woman who forgave. I was the kind of woman who believed in LOVE. Loving to the point of selflessness. I made the choice to go to the source of energy and love. I turned to my creator and I prayed for my spirit to let go of your spirit all together. In my solitude I prayed for strength to forgive you. I prayed for wisdom on how to handle my circumstances. I prayed for wisdom on how to control my emotions. After-all, what would have been the point of showing you what real love is supposed to be if I turned around and became just like you? When I took the steps to forgive you I began to see the blessings that were in store for me. I also realized there was a purpose behind all the heartache. I started to see myself clearly, the same way I learned to see you through your actions. Then, my hate turned to empathy and I did the inevitable, I prayed for you. The moment I allowed myself to speak blessings onto your life was, the same moment I felt my heart begin to heal.

The Ghost Of Me

Must be a treacherous thing,
Having to look at him,
And see pieces of me,
Lingering deep in his subconscious.
All the habits he learned with me,
Habits he won't set free.
All of my imperfections,
Mixed with all the greatness he found in me.
The world of my opinions,
Wrapped in the style of my idiosyncrasies.
All the songs that he still plays,
That calm the frustration I emote till this very day.
All the seeds I planted in his core,
All the things I did to make him soar.
All the truth I left in him,
That has left him slightly indebted,
With marks of me.
It's a pity,
For the woman who competes
With this ghost,
For in his mirror,
I haunt his soul.

Not A Toy

You want to play me,
I can see your moves.
Little do you know,
I'm not a toy.
This is not a game,
This is my heart you're fucking up.
Have I not been honest with my thoughts?
Have I not agreed to love you,
Even with your flaws?
So why lie?
When the truth is the necessary option.
You play vague,
When I throw at you questions.
Maybe I should throw knives and plates instead,
For you to get the memo!
Because what you're doing to my soul,
Is a crime of its own.
You're dragging me into a selfish war,
Then you wanna call it love.
Apparently destroying yourself is not enough.
And since my soul is tied to yours,
I am doomed if I don't let you go.
On occasions my heart you have destroyed,
I cannot let you do the same once more.

Tears

Her tears,
Ran helplessly out her eyes.
Pouring down her cheeks,
Inevitably touching her lips.
Only for her to realize,
That each drop still tastes like him.

Neruda, Was Right

Neruda was right.
Love is certainly short,
And forgetting you seems so long.

Neruda was right.
I love you,
Like dark things should be loved.
In secret between a dark shadow
And the soul.

Neruda was right,
I crave your mouth,
And I can't explain,
The simple pleasures
Your eyes bring to my face.

Neruda was right,
I need you tonight,
More than last night,
And the night before.

Neruda was right,
I go from loving you to not loving you,
From waiting to not waiting for you,
Living with the fate that today,
Like yesterday,

I still do not love you except because I still love you.

The Switch

A switch occurred,
In which I no longer feel the same.
I no longer hesitate
At the mention of your name.
The disappointment doesn't emote tears
In any way.
When I think of you,
I know I learned from my mistakes.
Of letting you back in again,
Without dismay.
You weaved in lies,
Like a spider's web.
Now I see the truth,
Clear as a cloudless day.
I'm as humble as they come,
But women like me are few and in between,
By now I'm sure you know,
I'm not the type
who looks the other way,
I confront the truth,
Even if it comes with shame.
You can call me crazy,
But you can't ever call me dumb.
For I'm the type who'll fight with bulls for what I love,
And loving myself is now in first place,
I no longer have time to deal with issues,
You never want to change.

LETTER XI

I believe longing made me love you more.
When you kissed me,
I felt my missing half returned at last.
Part of me finally feels alive.
If only we could make this last.
Without the past overshadowing,
The wonder you made me feel tonight.

Passion

Some cravings don't easily subside. Who would have thought all this time we were fighting the same battle? We had created a distance between us. We were both fighting the urge and the desire to be by each other's side again. It was months of wanting to hold each other and to stare into each other's eyes. Months in which we didn't allow our bodies to connect because we were both full of resentment. We hadn't exchanged more than a few words through text in an entire year. I buried you so deep into a dark abyss, even saying your name left a sour taste in my mouth. It's shocking what time can do, how two people who were once so close can later act as if the other was dead. Life always surprises you when you least expect it. One evening while visiting a friend in Paris I ran into you, the first time in a year. We were in what has to be one of the smallest restaurants in the city of lights. You stopped and looked at me, you didn't know what to do. Before I looked away we locked eyes, and in that brief moment your presence stirred my soul.

When we were in love I dreamt of visiting Paris with you. I dreamt of you kissing me on a high balcony, the city painted bright in the background. I dreamt of all the things hoped for by two people who loved each other. In difficult times and in better times. Sadly, we were in my favorite city, it was better times but we were now strangers. After all the history we shared, after everything we built, strangers. It seems that in that past year without you I had experienced so much, both lived amazing experiences apart; it's as if after you I had lived a thousand lives. *Yet why is it my most important life was the one I spent with you? Because there was no champagne, no city, or no man that could make me forget you. At the end of the day there was still you, there is always you.*

You began to contact me after our parisian encounter. At first I was cold. I didn't trust your intentions, although I did find pleasure in your words and in your guilt. I refused to see you on several occasions until eventually I gave in. Perhaps it was a bad idea, you had caused me so much pain. It is said that sometimes the greater the love, the greater the pain. You definitely did not deserve to see me, but I needed to answer some questions for myself. I needed to look into your eyes again. I needed to know if in your eyes there were remnants of any love left for me. I needed to quench my heart and give it the answer that for months it had been seeking. My heart needed to know if after all this time I still loved you.

I feared meeting you in public. I feared anyone we knew seeing us. So I made dinner just like how I used to. You always loved my cooking. Everyone assumed we hated each other. Our dinner was going to be my secret. Perhaps because I feared being judged or perhaps because I feared the outcome. I must admit that when I opened the door I was nervous and although a year had passed I still knew you well enough that I could smell the nervousness in you too. We sat across from each other looking out the same view of the Hollywood Hills in which we always used to sit by. I watched you eat your burrata salad as you told me stories of the food you ate in Italy last. It was interesting to hear you talk about your new experiences. You talked about wanting to live in different places and not wanting to be conformed to one place anymore. You sounded exactly like me. You sounded like the person years earlier you felt you were not good enough for. It was also interesting to see how openly you still spoke to me. I was secretly analyzing every part of you. I wanted to observe if time changed you and if time had changed me.

Hours later I allowed you to enter the bedroom that the ghost of you still haunted. I allowed you to touch me. There we were again, together in the bed where it all began. Anxiety filled me for I didn't know how to act. The moment you embraced me and I felt your warm body against mine, I knew you were my home. You kissed me passionately like a man who had been yearning for that moment, as if to devour me. Your hands began to travel landing on every point of my body. As if they were aware of how terribly my body missed them. I kissed your fingers and your knuckles until your fingerprints were left on every layer of my skin. Your lips tenderly found every freckle light or dark, seen or unseen. My skin belonged against yours and the sweat that escaped my pores had needed to mix with yours. That is the science that exists between us.

Some loves are like a disease. They stay dormant in your body until randomly a flare lights up, then it is spread through out your system, and you find yourself fighting against it all over again. You proved to be my disease and the following day I was left wondering if I had made a terrible mistake. It felt so right to make love to you and to let you love me. Yet I understood I had made the quintessential mistake of opening the door to an emotion I wasn't ready for again, all the pain you had put me through had weighed me down. Deep inside I hoped the bad parts of you would indeed change. God knows I had loved you desperately and I still wanted to continue loving you. Loving you in the same tragic way, if not greater. I started to question the relationship we had at one point, I questioned your return into my life. Although in the past I was blinded by resentment and hate. I concluded time didn't change the fact that I still loved you. When it comes to the heart what is time but the illusion of people changing. Time can be wrong. Time does not have to change the heart. When you touched me I still felt alive. My composition still reacted to your chemistry, proving that time is only but a factor. One which means nothing and nothing at all. I still wanted you, and I realized I would always love you.

Life is about full circles. When things are unfinished, one must be confident that time will bring the correct closure. I always knew you would come back, the same way they all came back. We still had unfinished business, we both needed our own personal closure. The weeks turned into months and with constant communication we listened to each other, we told each other everything we felt we needed to divulge. You perhaps did it for your own peace of mind and I did it in order to let go of any remaining resentment I carried with me in regards to our past. Yet you and I have a certain sexual familiarity that made it impossible for us not to continue having sex. In the end we know who we each desire more than anyone else. You know exactly how to take me to an orgasmic peak every time. And I know how to please you exactly the way you like. Sometimes the grass isn't greener on the other side.

At times I found myself fighting it, but your intensity would bring me back to you. The more sex I had with you only made it worse because it proved my desire to love you. You said you loved me more now then when we were together, *because after all our drama, all the hate we experienced you still loved me and would do anything for me.* But if in our story love was not enough, sex was definitely not enough either. You repeatedly said you had not changed very much since we separated. I felt you had grown in a business sense, you worked vigorously but you felt you still needed to experience more when it came to women. For now you had a larger appetite with less clarity, different girls in different cities, you had more options. I appreciated how you opened up to me. It was a different way of us communicating. I listened more than I reacted because I wasn't your partner anymore. I was simply a flawed woman figuring out where you fit in my life. One night after one of many conversations seeking a solution for what we were feeling, wondering how it could translate into the reality our lives were. I laid my head on the sea of white pillows that adorned the bed I still considered "ours", stared out the window observing the view of lights that flickered from afar, and one of my favorite songs came to mind, Guns

N' Roses vulnerable lyrics of "November Rain". At the end of the day unlike the other women you had in your life I knew what it was like to have you all for myself. There was no false sense of security and like the song says I can rest my head knowing that at some point in time you were truly all mine, and I was truly all yours. We were in sync, and we will always have that bond.

I don't know if I will ever have the chance at a greater love than ours. I don't know if you will love me forever as you once promised. I don't know if you will ever comprehend the way my heart still beats at the sound of your voice through the telephone wires. I don't know if you will ever understand how beautiful you are to me. I don't know if we will ever decide to continue our crazy story of love. What I do know is that our story put me through fire, and I survived. I became a full woman and proved to be stronger than the girl you had met so many years ago. I learned happiness was not fleeting, that I possessed the power to create it. That night without knowing if we would ever share a bed again I noticed I no longer slept on my side of the bed. Turns out that for some time I had been sleeping in the middle. I had learned to sleep in the middle of the bed, in the same way I allowed myself to heal from the pain.

Let's Pretend

Let's pretend you never said you love me,
And I'll pretend I didn't say that either.
Let's pretend that I don't dream of you,
And you can pretend that u don't either.
Let's pretend that you don't crave me,
And I'll pretend my body doesn't need you.
Let's pretend that we are strangers,
And our words travel but they miss us.
Let's pretend there is no hope,
And we are only but a box of memories,
With living traces,
Of a damaged love we carry in us.

Resurrection

There was burial a few months back.
I was head to toe in black.
Out of self-defense I killed a man.
I made it look like suicide.
I witnessed the soil seal his fate.
Convinced was I that he was dead.
But from his sleep he rose.
He resurrected to prove a point.
Stabbing my heart was not enough,
He now too desired my soul.

Dusk And Dawn

You and I are dusk and dawn.
Pitch dark,
Yet clear as the purest water.
We are night and day.
We need each other
In the same exact way.
I need you
How the night needs the day to rise.
You need me
How the day needs for the night to fall.
Our story is one of love.
A love that rises and that falls.
We rise and we fall.
With the same impossibility
The day and night suffer from.
We are gifted and cursed,
For we cannot dwell with each other.

Addiction

I was taught that drugs were bad.
I was taught to stay away,
To never try them, not once,
For drugs would dim my light.
I should never sacrifice my smile,
Especially for a temporary high.
When I met you,
I strayed away.
I took a hit,
And it has never been the same.
I must have injected you,
In my thickest vein.
My lungs must have inhaled you,
And it reached my brain.
My senses are now your slaves,
I seem to relapse every given day.
Because you live within me,
Like an addiction,
I cannot break from.
Every particle of you
Has mixed with my blood.
Every artery of mine,
Pumps your love.

Tainted Lovers

I want to give you,
Every part of my soul,
Even the broken pieces.
Because tainted is what I am.
Tainted is what you are.
Other lips have kissed my flesh,
But your lips kissed my heart.
Other hands caressed your face,
But my hands command your touch.
Confusion should be no more.
For tainted we must accept we are.
Tainted lovers are what we'll be.
For by your side I wish to be,
Even tainted,
That's okay with me.

The Rain

The rain always reminds me of you.
It was in the rain I first realized I was in love with you.
It is in the rain I make the best love to you.
There is nothing sad about the soundtrack
Of rain against the window pane.
The rain provides a certain peace.
The world slows down for you and me.
I hear your breathing more clearly,
The natural light has dimmed,
And shadows your body quite perfectly.
A storm arises,
As we lay over covers.
Wet off our own sweat,
As you plant kisses on my back,
And your hands take control of my waist.
You talk in my ear,
Say all the things I need to hear.
And the rain comes down,
Forming the backdrop to a perfect scenario,
Reminding me these are the moments,
That passionately,
                    last forever.

I Know About Us

I know about attraction
And about infatuation,
With some liquor action.
I know about those moments,
Full of questions,
And no answers.
Never enough,
Because I know about you,
And I know about me.
I know about us,
And how we can't seem
To let each other free.
This love is twisted,
An extreme affair.
Both hearts tied,
with unreasonable flair.
We attempt discretion,
Waiting for a solution to arise,
One with enough desire,
One that holds the bravest valor.
Since cowardly loves don't inherit kingdoms,
And real love must overshadow,
Failed seasons.

I Live You

I have swam against the currents of your love,
Fought against the power of your words.
Risen above the pain of a dark past,
And now I found myself surrendering to your touch.
Inhaling the aroma of your bodily scent,
And enjoying the decadence of your bottom lip.
Tracing with my lips the smoothness of your chest,
As you enchant me with your mind.
I have lived you within memory's frame
And if time is but a line,
One that goes forward and traces back.
I can see an infinite future
In which this love won't subside
And I shall continue on living you,
Like the stars live the night,
Even when the haze blocks their light.

Let It Kill Us

I don't know what I'm doing
Or why I'm pursuing
This love again with you.
I am probably only digging
The hole even deeper.
I am crawling around moments,
And your forever present eyes,
That never leave my mind,
But only linger.
I can't resist
The sensation of your touch,
As my insides explode,
At the mere stimulation
Of your fingers.
This is beyond lust,
You know how to manipulate my trust.
This is truly a fatal love,
And I succumb.
Here is the dagger,
Come,
Let it kill us.

Still

I've bounced back and forth from you,
Like a ball in a child's hands.
I've danced with you,
And away from you like a heroine in
A Shakespeare play.
And here I am counting breaths,
Sitting still on this corner bed.
Wondering if you'll ever comprehend,
Sometime girls stupidly,
Play pretend.
I still love you,
Even when I choose to walk away.
But on my life,
On you I'll never turn my back,
Even if that means I have to lose my pride
And scream at you,
To convince you to stay.

How Beautiful You Are To Me

I can chase the moon East
A hundred miles per hour.
Run dozens of red lights
Without any necessary caution.
And fear won't abide
As long as you are by my side.

I can drive through windy roads
In the South of France.
Panoramic views,
Straight out of movie screens.
And excitement won't exist
Unless it is you next to me.

I can swim through coral reefs,
And hike the tallest mountain peak,
Reach for stars that feel so close,
As if they are falling above me.
And nothing will compare

To how beautiful you are to me.

Let your pain empower you,
not all of us are destined to break.
And if you find yourself broken,
allow for each broken piece

to faithfully make sense.

Hope

There is a pivotal moment in all of our lives when we have to make decisions for our own sanity. Decisions that shine light on the difference between desire and need. I began to make definitive decisions for my future when I learned to place myself first. How can I give to others if I'm not whole? I made the decision of cutting ties with people that weren't making me better. I took time to travel and focus on my relationship with myself. I paid attention to my needs, my dreams and my goals. A year of soul searching and I reached a point in which I needed to understand where love fits after a breakup, after a loss. Eventually I realized that real love never stops. Torrents will crash, rivers will flood and eventually dry up, but love remains underneath it all. When people part ways where does the love go? It can subside but it goes nowhere.

I will always love the men I loved once. My love was real and strong for them, and although time will not change that, love is an energy that can change its form. I respect them, and will forever hope the best for them. I will remember our stories without the need to relive them. For stories can never be duplicated, they must remain what they were, and one must remain with the hope and desire of living out other stories as well. After love life does not stop. Life keeps on going. It's up to us to create the story we want to live. I made mistakes and lived through them. I survived loss and it made me stronger. I loved and it made me better. Through my failures I found my greatness. In that process I can say I learned the true essence of what love is. I learned of the amount of love I can give. I learned that maybe it takes a brave man to be with a woman like me. I learned that in relationships I don't look the other way. I don't dim my voice when I have something to say. I learned that I don't do well with huge egos for I will always see myself as his equal. I learned about the type of love I want and deserve. Most importantly I accepted the fact that I am woman who believes in love. In the type of love that survives obstacles. The type of love that is treasurable because it's polished in pain. The type of love that is vibrant enough to palpitate through every vein in my body. The type of love that owns my smile and joy combined. The type of love that gives to the point of pure selflessness. The type of love I'll never want to live without. I don't know what the future will bring or what route my life will take, but every morning I wake up believing that type of love will find me someday. I will not lose hope, I refuse to settle for anything less.

Ready

Your eyes speak volumes,
To the type of woman I yearn to be.
While your words,
Speak greatness into me.
Your handshake counts,
In era in which character is almost extinct.
You walk into a room,
And your presence alone commands respect.
I observe how eloquently you express yourself.
Your style is simple, with an impeccable taste.
You watch your voice,
And have knowledge of the powerof your words.
Both my heart and mind admire you effortlessly.
I thank God and the heavens
For every failed love,
For every fire that burnt me,
For every obstacle encountered,
For in that pain I was polished,
Ready to love and be loved by you.

September Leaves

The weather changed
After you left.
It's no longer warm,
And the wind
Now has traces of cold in it.
The leaves are turning brown,
And falling by the minute.
The sun still shines,
But its brightness
Is decreasing daily.
For it is the beginning
Of a new season.
Yet my heart sinks in fear
That like the summer,
The memory of us
Will begin to fade,
And we won't exist,
Just like the leaves that will soon
Need to be raked away.

Desire

I want to study every corner
Of your body,
All of which that makes you whole.
I want to find every key
For every secret
You keep behind closed doors.
I want to memorize
The variety of your expressions,
Just as if they were my own.
I want to read your eyes
And know when your pupils dilate,
The moment they meet attraction.
I want to know you inside out
To the point I become the only
source of your arousal.

I'm Never Good At First Dates

I'm never good at first dates,
I talk too much,
Look away when his eyes find mine.
I release awkward smiles.
Smiles that introduce him to the twelve year old in me.
Smiles that coyly answer the questions
He discreetly asked from me.

I'm never good at first dates,
And a man who rapidly tries to hold my hand.
I've never been good at holding hands,
As if giving ownership of me.
You see, I'm jealous with myself,
Too many tears have been shed,
To set my inner goddess free.

I'm never good at first dates,
I must keep these walls up,
Until he fights enough,
For me to let him in.
I have issues this I know,
But these issues make me strong.
They protect my mind and soul,
From the corruption of a shallow world.

The Taste Of You

The taste of you
Remains on the very surface
Of my lips.
The touch of your hands
Passionately lingers
Like a present dream.
You awoke a certain heat,
On every layer of my skin.
Now there is a flame,
One that burns,
Deep and ardently
Inside of me.

Sorry, If I'm Blasphemous

People do the craziest things for religion.
Cover themselves from head to toe,
In the heat of the desert.
Lives will revolve around not one
But several prayer clocks.
They will change their environments,
And eating habits.
Some will only pick up books
That strengthen their unbreakable faith,
While others go door to door
Spreading their beliefs.
I on the other hand am selfish,
For I want to be the only religion
You seek comfort in.
I want to inspire you in not one but many changes,
Because you have faith
In the goddess that lives in me.
May all your clocks
Revolve around us,
Because you were reborn
When you found my love.
Sorry if I'm being blasphemous,
But I want you extremely religious.
So religious,
That you'll do the craziest things,
To satisfy the need
Of proving your love to me.

Dream World

Every night I enter a world,
Full of flowers.
Out of all the flowers,
The most powerful scent
Is always you.
In that world I live out stories,
Every night the setting changes,
Sometimes the plot thickens,
But what always remains constant
Is that you darling,
Are always in it.
For in these stories
You are the protagonist,
You are the hero that saves my day.
You are my knight
In shining armor,
Why wouldn't I want to enter
That dream world everyday?

Must Confess

I must confess,
I am insatiable for your love.
There are urges in my body,
That are full of you.
Cravings that possess every letter of your name,
And such desires seem to have no end.

Love Letter

Tell me you love me with your eyes,
For they hold the truth of your inner soul.
Tell me you love me with your touch,
So I can engrave it deep under my pores.
Tell me you love me with your actions,
Move mountains, sands, and sea,
Everything and anything you must do
To show your love to me.
Tell me you love me with your mouth,
And turn those words into writing,
To prove to every skeptic,
                              Love letters still exist.

Acknowledgments

My first attempt at writing a book began at twenty-three. My second attempt at twenty-five. My third attempt at twenty-eight which became "Letters, To The Men I have loved". Staying focused was the most essential element in finishing this time around. I couldn't have accomplished that without the support of a number of people. First of all I am thankful to God for giving me the love of words. Thank you for always guarding my steps and for always showing me the light at the end of the tunnel. I'd like to thank my parents Jose R. Castro and Mirtha J. Castro-Mármol for being my emotional and spiritual support during this process. I love you both so much. I'd like to thank my siblings Cathryn and Jose Angel Castro Mármol. Your positivity has always motivated me through out the years. I am proud and love both of you dearly. My Pyro Anthony Jules thank you for being you. Everything I do is for you.

All the poems were written through out a nine-year period while the letters took seven months to write. Certain friends were an incredible help with my weekly progress to envision the possibilities and to market the book. Thank you Kristen Noel Gipson for believing and motivating me when I was in a professional rut. Thank you for staying on the phone with me for hours listening to my ideas, and lifting me up. You envisioned this book when I first spoke to you about it. You were my first friend to promote me. You have proven to be a blessing in my life and I am very grateful for your friendship. Fanny Bourdette-Donon, not only are you the most elegant and chic human being in my life and have influenced my life in many ways, but the support you gave me during this time in my life I will never forget. You are in another continent and always available. Thank you for our decade long friendship and all the expertise you provided me through out different career ventures in my life. I am forever grateful. Thank you Michelle Kong, my Chinese Jamaican Thai Goddess. You know about every man that has walked into my life since I was thirteen years old. I have lived some of my best experiences with you. You know what I'm thinking before I say it. We have a bond that no one or time can break. Dayana Ariza, Lauren Rodriguez, Ydalia Cejas my high school sweethearts. We are older now, two of you are married to great men, and the other is engaged to a great one as well. You guys were my sanity and my reality check in Miami and after I left Miami. You girls are family to me and I am so proud of the amazing women you have become. Thank you for being part of my foundation and always being a call away. Surina Phangura, I'll never forget how you were my rock during the worst break up I ever experienced. My life fell apart and you always brought laughter when I needed it the most, Piyar! Tiffany Barras, Heidi-Marie, Assal Deshmeh, France Falcon, Frankie Nicole, Susan Carvajal, Cassie Santana, Julissa Guzman, Cande Quiroga. All of you ladies have been my support system at different times in my life. I became a woman with all of you girls. You listened to my problems. You took me out when I was depressed. You took care of me when I drank too much. You made me laugh when I needed it the most. You helped me when times were hard. You hugged me when I cried. You pushed me to succeed in different projects. You listened to my poetry when no one knew I was a poet. You inspired me and continue to do so. You are the best friends any girl can ask for. Thank you for sharing with me your greatness.

I'd like to thank certain relatives for your influence in my life through out the years. My grandmother Mercedes Dimeris Mármol, Tia Eloisa, Tio Angel, Tio Dario, Tia Sonia, Tia Luz Virginia, Tia Loida, Tia Viviana, Karen, Cynthia, Ryan, Angel Alberto, Joel, Jennifer, Angelissa, Angie, Sonia Elizabeth, Manuelcito, Rosa, Ana Zunilda, Alex, Diana Carolina, Cristian Garza, Maritza Encarnacion, Stephanie, Eric, Tia Ana, Tio Dario, Bianca, Carolina, Jose Daniel Baez.

Thank you Jerry Meng for being such an amazing friend. You are efficient, smart, loving, supportive and loyal. This book would not have seen the light of day without your immense help. I am extremely blessed to have you in my life. Thank Ibn Jasper and Q. Ladraa. I had a lunch with the both of you when I began to write the book. Both of you motivated me to do it myself. To self publish and to be fearless. Thank you Henrique Belisle, your middle name should have been fabulous. Your heart is so big and your soul is pure. God blessed me when I met you. Thank you Mike G for being such a great friend and confidant. You always give the best male advice. I love and appreciate you. Thank you to the following people who make my life better and supported me with the release of this book. Victor Alexander Barco, Aureta Thomolari, Cherin Choi, Zahra Ayub, Margaret Garabet, Jen Gomez, Sylvain Bitton, Zulay Henao, Jamie Baratta, Neran Dhas, Jhonathan Duarte, Yaritza Caraballo, Eli Mizrahi, Jacob Freed, Olivier Rousteing. You guys rock Love you! Thank you to my friend and agent Cameron Mitchell for believing in me and fighting for me. I love and appreciate you! Rob, together or not, I'm glad the love we have for each other was stronger than any of our differences. You have been such an important part of my journey. I am grateful for our story. Love you flaco.